To:

....

From:

....

Grace Happens Here™

YOU ARE STANDING WHERE
GRACE IS HAPPENING

MAX LUCADO

THOMAS NELSON
Since 1798

NASHVILLE   DALLAS   MEXICO CITY   RIO DE JANEIRO   BEIJING

Published in Nashville, Tennessee, by Thomas Nelson®. Thomas Nelson is a registered trademark of Thomas Nelson, Inc.

Thomas Nelson, Inc., titles may be purchased in bulk for educational, business, fundraising, or sales promotional use. For information, please e-mail SpecialMarkets@ThomasNelson.com.

Cover design by LeftCoast Design

Compiled by Terri Gibbs

iStock and Shutterstock photo credits are listed at the back of the book

Unless otherwise noted, Scripture quotations are taken from HOLY BIBLE: NEW INTERNATIONAL VERSION®. © 1993, 1978, 1984 by International Bible Society. Used by permission of Zondervan Publishing House. All rights reserved. Scripture quotations marked MSG are from *The Message* by Eugene H. Peterson. © 1993, 1994, 1995, 1996, 2000. Used by permission of NavPress Publishing Group. All rights reserved. Scripture quotations marked NCV are from the New Century Version®. © 2005 by Thomas Nelson, Inc. Used by permission. All rights reserved. Scripture quotations marked NLT are from the *Holy Bible*, New Living Translation. © 1996, 2004. Used by permission of Tyndale House Publishers, Inc., Wheaton, Illinois 60189. All rights reserved. Scripture quotations marked NASB are from NEW AMERICAN STANDARD BIBLE ®. © 1960, 1962, 1963, 1968, 1971, 1973, 1975, 1977, 1995 by The Lockman Foundation. Scripture quotations marked NKJV are taken from THE NEW KING JAMES VERSION®. © 1982 by Thomas Nelson, Inc. Used by permission. All rights reserved.

ISBN-13: 978-1-4003-2038-7

Printed in Mexico

12 13 14 15 [QG] 5 4 3 2

CONTENTS

PURSUED
BY
Grace

To discover grace

is to discover God's utter devotion to you,
his stubborn resolve to give you a

cleansing,
healing,
purging love
that lifts the wounded
back to their feet.

GOD GIVES A NEW HEART

When grace happens, we receive not a nice compliment from God but a new heart. Give your heart to Christ, and he returns the favor. "I will give you a new heart and put a new spirit within you" (Ezekiel 36:26 NKJV).

You might call it a spiritual heart transplant.

Tara Storch understands this miracle as much as anyone can. In the spring of 2010, a skiing accident took the life of her thirteen-year-old daughter, Taylor. What followed for Tara and her husband, Todd, was every parent's worst nightmare: a funeral, a burial, a flood of questions and tears. They decided to donate their daughter's organs to needy patients. Few people needed a heart more than Patricia Winters. Her heart had begun to fail five years earlier, leaving her too weak to do much more than sleep. Taylor's heart gave Patricia a fresh start on life.

Tara had only one request: she wanted to hear the heart of her daughter. She and Todd flew from Dallas to Phoenix and went to Patricia's home to listen to Taylor's heart.

The two mothers embraced for a long time. Then Patricia offered Tara and Todd a stethoscope. When they listened to the healthy rhythm, whose heart did they hear? Did they not hear the still-beating heart of their daughter? It indwells a different body, but the heart is the heart of their child. And when God hears your heart, does he not hear the still-beating heart of his Son? . . .

The Christian is a person in whom Christ is happening.

—*Grace*

God dispenses his goodness not with an eyedropper but a fire hydrant.

Your heart is a Dixie cup, and his grace is the Mediterranean Sea.

You simply can't contain it all.

BUT YOU, O LORD, ARE A COMPASSIONATE
AND GRACIOUS GOD,
SLOW TO ANGER, ABOUNDING IN
LOVE AND FAITHFULNESS.

Psalm 86:15

God wrote the book on grace.
He coaxed Adam and Eve out of
the bushes, murderous Moses out
of the desert. He made a place for
David, though David made a move
on Bathsheba. He didn't give up on
Elijah, though Elijah gave up on him.
Undeserved. Unexpected. Grace.

BEFORE WE KNEW OUR NEED

The bank sent me an overdraft notice on the checking account of one of my daughters. I encouraged my college-age girls to monitor their accounts. Even so, they sometimes overspent.

What should I have done? Let the bank absorb it? They wouldn't. Send her an angry letter? Admonition might have helped her later, but it wouldn't satisfy the bank. Phone and tell her to make a deposit? Might as well tell a fish to fly. I knew her liquidity. Zero.

Transfer the money from my account to hers? Seemed to be the best option. After all, I had $25.37. I could have replenished her account and paid the overdraft fee as well.

Besides, that was my job. Don't get any ideas. If you're overdrawn, don't call me. My daughter can do something you can't do: she can call me Dad. And since she calls me Dad, I did what dads do. I covered my daughter's mistake.

When I told her she was overdrawn, she said she was sorry. Still, she offered no deposit. She was broke. She had one option. "Dad, could you . . ." I interrupted her sentence. "Honey, I already have." I met her need before she knew she had one.

Long before you knew you needed grace, your Father did the same. He made the deposit, an ample deposit: "Christ died for us while we were still sinners" (Romans 5:8 NCV). Before you knew you needed a Savior, you had one. And when you ask him for mercy, he answers, "I've already given it, dear child. I've already given it."

—*Cure for the Common Life*

Jesus

treats your shame-filled days

with grace.

He'll take your guilt
if you'll ask him.

All he awaits is your request.

We cup sullied hearts in hands
and offer them to God
as we would a crushed, scentless flower:

"Can you bring life to this?"
And he does.

It was not with perishable things such as silver or gold that you were redeemed from the empty way of life handed down to you from your forefathers, but with the precious blood of Christ, a lamb without blemish or defect.

1 Peter 1:18–19

GRACE FOR BREAKFAST

Peter's thoughts are interrupted by a shout from the shore. "Catch any fish?"

Peter and John look up. Probably a villager. "No!" they yell.

"Try the other side!" the voice yells back.

John looks at Peter. What harm? So out sails the net. Peter wraps the rope around his wrist to wait.

But there is no wait. The rope pulls taut, and the net catches. Peter sets his weight against the side of the boat and begins to bring in the net. He's so intense with the task, he misses the message.

John doesn't. The moment is déjà vu. This has happened before. The long night. The empty net. The call to cast again. Fish flapping on the floor of the boat. Wait a minute . . . He lifts his eyes to the man on the shore. "It's him," he whispers.

Then louder, "It's Jesus."

Peter turns and looks. Jesus, the God of heaven and earth, is on the shore . . . and he's building a fire.

Peter plunges into the water, swims to the shore, and stumbles out wet and shivering and stands in front of the friend he betrayed. Jesus has prepared a bed of coals.

For one of the few times in his life, Peter is silent. What words would suffice? The moment is too holy for words. God is offering breakfast to the friend who betrayed him. And Peter is once again finding grace at Galilee.

What do you say at a moment like this?

What do you say at a moment such as this?

It's just you and God. You and God both know what you did. And neither one of you is proud of it. What do you do?

You might consider doing what Peter did. Stand in God's presence. Stand in his sight. Stand still and wait. Sometimes that's all a soul can do. Too repentant to speak, but too hopeful to leave—we just stand.

Stand amazed.

He has come back.

He invites you to try again. This time, with him.

—3:16, *Numbers of Hope*

We are
presumptuous
not when we
marvel at God's
grace, but when
we reject it.

God offers
second chances,
like a soup kitchen
offers meals,

to everyone
who asks.

PEOPLE CANNOT DO ANY WORK THAT
WILL MAKE THEM RIGHT WITH GOD.

Romans 4:5 NCV

Salvation is the result of grace.

⟡⟡

Without exception,
no man or woman has ever
done one work to enhance

the finished work
of the cross.

OUR HEAVENLY FATHER GIVES GRACE

Come with me to God's living room.

Sit in the chair that was made for you and warm your hands by the fire which never fades. . . . Stand at the mantel and study the painting which hangs above it.

Your Father treasures the portrait. He has hung it where all can see. . . .

Captured in the portrait is a tender scene of a father and a son. Behind them is a great house on a hill. Beneath their feet is a narrow path. Down from the house the father has run. Up the trail the son has trudged. The two have met, here, at the gate.

We can't see the face of the son; it's buried in the chest of his father. No, we can't see his face, but we can see his tattered robe and stringy hair. We can see the mud on the back of his legs, the filth on his shoulders and the empty purse on the ground. At one time the purse was full of money. At one time the boy was full of pride. But that was a dozen taverns ago. Now both the purse and the pride are depleted. The prodigal offers no gift or explanation. All he offers is the smell of pigs and a rehearsed apology: "Father, I have sinned against God and against you. I am no longer worthy to be called your son" (Luke 15:21 NCV). . . .

Though we can't see the boy's face in the painting, we can't miss the father's. Look at the tears glistening on the leathered cheeks, the smile shining through the silver beard. One arm holds the boy up so he won't fall, the other holds the boy close so he won't doubt.

"Hurry!" he shouts. "Bring the best clothes and put them on him. Also, put a ring on his finger and sandals on his feet. And get our fat calf and kill it so we can have a feast and celebrate. My son was dead, but now he is alive again! He was lost but now he is found!" (Luke 15:22–24 NCV). . . .

Gaze at this painting and be reminded of your God: It is right to call him Holy; we speak truth when we call him King. But if you want to touch his heart, use the name he loves to hear. Call him *Father*.

—*The Great House of God*

Christ came to earth for one reason:
to give his life as a ransom

❧❧

for you,
for me,
for all of us.

He sacrificed himself
to give us a second chance.

HE WAS WOUNDED FOR THE WRONG WE DID;
HE WAS CRUSHED FOR THE EVIL WE DID.

Isaiah 53:5 NCV

Have you ever been given a gift
that compares to God's grace?

Finding this treasure
of mercy makes the
poorest beggar a prince.

Missing this gift makes the
wealthiest man a pauper.

GOD'S GRACIOUS LOVE

At the time Martin Luther was having his Bible printed in Germany, a printer's daughter encountered God's love. No one had told her about Jesus. Toward God she felt no emotion but fear. One day she gathered fallen pages of Scripture from the floor. On one paper she found the words "For God so loved the world, that he gave . . ." The rest of the verse had not yet been printed. Still, what she saw was enough to move her. The thought that God would give anything moved her from fear to joy. Her mother noticed the change of attitude.

When asked the cause of her happiness, the daughter produced the crumpled piece of partial verse from her pocket. The mother read it and asked, "What did he give?" The child was perplexed for a moment and then answered, "I do not know. But if He loved us well enough to give us anything, we should not be afraid of Him."[1]

—It's Not About Me

For God so loved the world that he gave his one and only Son, that whoever believes in him shall not perish but have eternal life.

John 3:16

Of all the things you must earn in life,

God's unending affection

is not one of them.

You have it.

Stretch yourself out in the hammock of grace.

You can rest now.

YOUR HEARTS SHOULD BE
STRENGTHENED BY GOD'S
GRACE, NOT BY OBEYING RULES.

Hebrews 13:9 NCV

We ask for *grace,* only to find *forgiveness* already offered.

SAVING

Grace

Jesus already knows the cost of grace.

He already knows the price of forgiveness.

But he offers it anyway.

❦

GOD DEMONSTRATES
HIS OWN LOVE FOR US IN
THIS: WHILE WE WERE
STILL SINNERS, CHRIST
DIED FOR US.

Romans 5:8

God didn't look at our frazzled lives and say,

"I'll die for you
when you deserve it."

No, despite our sin,
in the face of our rebellion,

.... ❧❧ ....

he chose to adopt us.

JESUS DIED FOR OUR SINS

As a young boy, I read a Russian fable about a master and a servant who went on a journey to a city. Many of the details I've forgotten, but the ending I remember. Before the two men could reach the destination, they were caught in a blinding blizzard. They lost their direction and were unable to reach the city before nightfall.

The next morning concerned friends went searching for the two men. They finally found the master, frozen to death, face down in the snow. When they lifted him they found the servant—cold but alive. He survived and told how the master had voluntarily placed himself on top of the servant so the servant could live.

I hadn't thought of that story in years. But when I read what Christ said he would do for us, the story surfaced—for Jesus is the master who died for the servants.

—And the Angels Were Silent

I WAS GIVEN MERCY SO
THAT IN ME, THE WORST
OF ALL SINNERS, CHRIST
JESUS COULD SHOW
THAT HE HAS PATIENCE
WITHOUT LIMIT.

1 Timothy 1:16 NCV

Our Savior kneels down and gazes
upon the darkest acts of our lives.
But rather than recoil in horror, he
reaches out in kindness and says,

"I can clean that if you want."

And from the basin of his grace,
he scoops a palm full of mercy and
washes away our sin.

Our faith does not earn God's love

any more than
our stupidity
jeopardizes it.

The cross was heavy, the blood was real,
and the price was extravagant.
It would have bankrupted you or me,
so he paid it for us.

Call it simple. Call it a gift.
But don't call it easy.

Call it what it is. Call it grace.

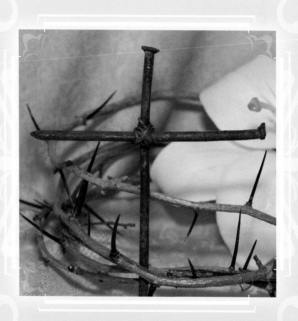

OUR PENALTY IS PAID

Back in our elementary school days, my brother received a BB gun for Christmas. We immediately set up a firing range in the backyard and spent the afternoon shooting at an archery target. Growing bored with the ease of hitting the circle, my brother sent me to fetch a hand mirror. He placed the gun backward on his shoulder, spotted the archery bull's-eye in the mirror, and did his best Buffalo Bill imitation. But he missed the target. He also missed the storehouse behind the target and the fence behind the storehouse. We had no idea where the BB pellet flew. Our neighbor across the alley knew, however. He soon appeared at the back fence, asking who had shot the BB gun and who was going to pay for his sliding-glass door.

At this point I disowned my brother. I changed my last name and claimed to be a holiday visitor from Canada.

My father was more noble than I. Hearing the noise, he appeared in the backyard, freshly rousted from his Christmas Day nap, and talked with the neighbor.

Among his words were these:

"Yes, they are my children."

"Yes, I'll pay for their mistakes."

Christ says the same about you. He knows you miss the target. He knows you can't pay for your mistakes. But he can. "God presented Jesus as the sacrifice for sin" (Romans 3:25 NLT).

—*Facing Your Giants*

To be saved by grace

is to be saved by

Jesus——

not by an idea, doctrine, creed, or church membership,

but by Jesus himself,

who will sweep into heaven anyone who so much as gives him the nod.

IF WE WALK IN THE LIGHT
AS HE IS IN THE LIGHT, WE
HAVE FELLOWSHIP WITH ONE
ANOTHER, AND THE BLOOD
OF JESUS CHRIST HIS SON
CLEANSES US FROM ALL SIN.

1 John 1:7 NKJV

God didn't overlook your sins,
lest he endorse them.

He didn't punish you,
lest he destroy you.

He instead found a way to punish the
sin and preserve the sinner.

Jesus took your punishment, and God
gave you credit for Jesus' perfection.

A SINNER SAVED BY GRACE

John had served on the seas since he was eleven years old. His father, an English shipmaster in the Mediterranean, took him aboard and trained him well for a life in the Royal Navy.

Yet what John gained in experience, he lacked in discipline. He mocked authority. Ran with the wrong crowd. Indulged in the sinful ways of a sailor. Although his training would have qualified him to serve as an officer, his behavior caused him to be flogged and demoted.

In his early twenties, he made his way to Africa, where he became intrigued by the lucrative slave trade. At age twenty-one, he made his living on the *Greyhound*, a slave ship crossing the Atlantic Ocean.

John ridiculed the moral and poked fun at the religious. He even made jokes about a book that would eventually help reshape his life: *The Imitation of Christ*. In fact, he was degrading that book a few hours before his ship sailed into an angry storm.

That night the waves pummeled the *Greyhound*, spinning the ship one minute on the top of a wave. Plunging her the next into a watery valley.

John awakened to find his cabin filled with water. A side of the *Greyhound* had collapsed. Ordinarily such damage would have sent a ship to the bottom in a matter of minutes. The *Greyhound*, however, was carrying buoyant cargo and remained afloat.

John worked at the pumps all night. For nine hours, he and the other sailors struggled to keep the ship from sinking. But he knew that it was a losing cause. Finally, when his hopes were more battered than the vessel, he threw himself on the saltwater-soaked deck and pleaded, "If this will not do, then Lord have mercy on us all."

John didn't deserve mercy, but he received it. The *Greyhound* and her crew survived.

John never forgot God's mercy shown on that tempestuous day on the roaring Atlantic. He returned to England where he became a powerful pulpiteer and a prolific composer. You've sung his songs, like this one:

Amazing grace! how sweet the sound,
That saved a wretch like me!

This slave-trader-turned-songwriter was John Newton. During his last years, someone asked him about his health. He confessed that his powers were failing. "My memory is almost gone," he said, "but I remember two things: I am a great sinner, and Jesus is a great Savior."

—*In the Eye of the Storm*

Salvation is God's business.

Grace

is his idea,
his work, and
his expense.

Attempts at self-salvation guarantee nothing but exhaustion.

FOR IT IS BY GRACE YOU HAVE BEEN SAVED,
THROUGH FAITH—AND THIS NOT FROM
YOURSELVES, IT IS THE GIFT OF GOD—NOT BY
WORKS, SO THAT NO ONE CAN BOAST.

Ephesians 2:8–9

You think God
would love
you more if
you did more,
right?

You think if you were
better, his love would
be deeper, right?

Wrong.

PARDONED BY GRACE

During the early days of the Civil War, a Union soldier was arrested on charges of desertion. Unable to prove his innocence, he was condemned and sentenced to die a deserter's death. His appeal found its way to the desk of Abraham Lincoln. The president felt mercy for the soldier and signed a pardon. The soldier returned to service, fought the entirety of the war, and was killed in the last battle. Found in his breast pocket was the signed letter of the president.

Close to the heart of the soldier were his leader's words of pardon. He found courage in grace. I wonder how many thousands more have found courage in the emblazoned cross of their heavenly king.

—In the Grip of Grace

Grace is everything Jesus.

···············❧···············

Grace lives because he does,
works because he works,
and matters because he matters.

·············❦·············

You can't be
good enough to
deserve forgiveness.

That's why
we need
a savior.

TRUSTING GOD'S GRACE

You need to trust God's grace.

Follow the example of the Chilean miners. Trapped beneath two thousand feet of solid rock, the thirty-three men were desperate. The collapse of a main tunnel had sealed their exit and thrust them into survival mode. They ate two spoonfuls of tuna, a sip of milk, and a morsel of peaches—every other day. For two months they prayed for someone to save them.

On the surface above, the Chilean rescue team worked around the clock, consulting NASA, meeting with experts. They designed a thirteen-foot-tall capsule and drilled, first a communication hole, then an excavation tunnel. There was no guarantee of success. No one had ever been trapped underground this long and lived to tell about it.

Now someone has.

On October 13, 2010, the men began to emerge, slapping high fives and leading victory chants. A great-grandfather. A forty-four-year-old who was planning a wedding. Then a nineteen-year-old. All had different stories, but all had made the same decision. They trusted someone else to save them. No one returned the rescue offer with a declaration of independence: "I can get out of here on my own. Just give me a new drill." They had stared at the stone tomb long enough to reach the unanimous opinion: "We need help. We need someone to penetrate this world and pull us out." And when the rescue capsule came, they climbed in.

Why is it so hard for us to do the same?

We find it easier to trust the miracle of resurrection than the miracle of grace. We so fear failure that we create the image of perfection, lest heaven be even more disappointed in us than we are. The result? The weariest people on earth.

Attempts at self-salvation guarantee nothing but exhaustion. We scamper and scurry, trying to please God, collecting merit badges and brownie points, and scowling at anyone who questions our accomplishments. Call us the church of hound-dog faces and slumped shoulders.

Stop it! Once and for all, enough of this frenzy. "Your hearts should be strengthened by God's grace, not by obeying rules" (Hebrews 13:9 NCV). Jesus does not say, "Come to me, all you who are perfect and sinless." Just the opposite. "Come to Me, all who are weary and heavy-laden, and I will give you rest" (Matthew 11:28 NASB).

—*Grace*

If you haven't accepted God's forgiveness, you are doomed to fear.

❖❖

You may deaden the fear, but you can't remove it.

Only God's grace can.

Jesus loves us too
much to leave us in
doubt about his grace.

He keeps no list
of our wrongs.

Let grace
trump your
arrest record,
critics,
and guilty conscience.

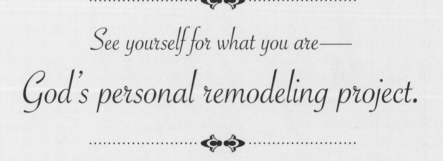

See yourself for what you are—

God's personal remodeling project.

Not a world to yourself
but a work in his hands.

CHANGED

BY

Grace

God works
the miracle of salvation.

❖❖

He immerses us
in mercy.

He stitches
together
our shredded
souls.

God's grace changes us,
shapes us, and leads us to a
life that is eternally altered.

THOUGH WE WERE
SPIRITUALLY DEAD
BECAUSE OF THE THINGS
WE DID AGAINST GOD, HE
GAVE US NEW LIFE WITH
CHRIST. YOU HAVE BEEN
SAVED BY GOD'S GRACE.

Ephesians 2:5 NCV

GOD CHANGES HEARTS

Some years ago I underwent a heart procedure. My heartbeat had the regularity of a telegraph operator sending Morse code. Fast, fast fast. Slooooow. After several failed attempts to restore healthy rhythm with medication, my doctor decided I should have a catheter ablation. The plan went like this: a cardiologist would insert two cables in my heart via a blood vessel. One was a camera; the other was an ablation tool. To ablate is to burn. Yes, burn, cauterize, singe, brand. If all went well, the doctor, to use his coinage, would destroy the "misbehaving" parts of my heart.

As I was being wheeled into surgery, he asked if I had any final questions. (Not the best choice of words.) I tried to be witty.

"You're burning the interior of my heart, right?"

"Correct."

"You intend to kill the misbehaving cells, yes?"

"That is my plan."

"As long as you are in there, could you take your little blowtorch to some of my greed, selfishness, superiority, and guilt?"

He smiled and answered, "Sorry, that's out of my pay grade."

Indeed it was, but it's not out of God's. He is in the business of changing hearts.

We would be wrong to think this change happens overnight. But we would be equally wrong to assume change never happens at all. It may come in fits and spurts—an "aha" here, a breakthrough there. But it comes. "The grace of God that brings salvation has appeared" (Titus 2:11 NKJV). The floodgates are open, and the water is out. You just never know when grace will seep in.

Could you use some?

—*Grace*

Grace is God's best idea.

.... ◆◇◆ ....

Rather than tell us to change, he creates the change.

Do we clean up so he can accept us? No, he accepts us and begins cleaning us up.

LET US THEN APPROACH
THE THRONE OF GRACE
WITH CONFIDENCE, SO
THAT WE MAY RECEIVE
MERCY AND FIND
GRACE TO HELP US IN
OUR TIME OF NEED.

Hebrews 4:16

Grace is the voice that calls us to change and then gives us the power to pull it off.

CHANGED BY GRACE

Victor Hugo introduced us to Jean Valjean in the classic *Les Misérables*. Valjean enters the pages as a vagabond. A just-released prisoner in midlife, wearing threadbare trousers and a tattered jacket. Nineteen years in a French prison have left him rough and fearless. He's walked for four days in the Alpine chill of nineteenth-century southeastern France, only to find that no inn will take him, no tavern will feed him. Finally he knocks on the door of a bishop's house.

Monseigneur Myriel is seventy-five years old. Like Valjean, he has lost much. The revolution took all the valuables from his family except some silverware, a soup ladle, and two candlesticks. Valjean tells his story and expects the religious man to turn him away. But the bishop is kind. He asks the visitor to sit near a fire.

"You did not need to tell me who you were," he explains. "This is not my house—it is the house of Jesus Christ."[2] After some time the bishop takes the ex-convict to the table, where they dine on soup and bread, figs, and cheese with wine, using the bishop's fine silverware.

He shows Valjean to a bedroom. In spite of the comfort, the ex-prisoner can't sleep. In spite of the kindness of the bishop, he can't resist the temptation. He stuffs the silverware into his knapsack. The priest sleeps through the robbery, and Valjean runs into the night.

But he doesn't get far. The policemen catch him and march him back to the bishop's house. Valjean knows what his capture means—prison for the rest of his life. But then something wonderful happens. Before the officer can explain the crime, the bishop steps forward.

"Oh! Here you are! I'm so glad to see you. I can't believe you forgot the candlesticks! They are made of pure silver as well. . . . Please take them with the forks and spoons I gave you."

Valjean is stunned. The bishop dismisses the policemen and then turns and says, "Jean Valjean, my brother, you no longer belong to evil, but to good. I have bought your soul from you. I take it back from evil thoughts and deeds and the Spirit of Hell, and I give it to God."[3]

Valjean has a choice: believe the priest or believe his past. Jean Valjean believes the priest. He becomes the mayor of a small town. He builds a factory and gives jobs to the poor. . . .

Grace changed him. Let it change you.

—Grace

To see sin without
grace is despair.
To see grace
without sin is
arrogance. To see
them in tandem is
conversion.

I HAVE BEEN CRUCIFIED WITH CHRIST AND I NO LONGER LIVE, BUT CHRIST LIVES IN ME. THE LIFE I LIVE IN THE BODY, I LIVE BY FAITH IN THE SON OF GOD, WHO LOVED ME AND GAVE HIMSELF FOR ME.

Galatians 2:20

Christ is on the move,
aggressively budging you from
graceless to grace-shaped living.
The gift-given giving gifts.

YOU ARE GOD'S MASTERPIECE

God sees in you a masterpiece about to happen.

He will do with you what Vik Muniz did with the garbage pickers of Gramacho. Jardim Gramacho is the largest landfill in the world, the Godzilla of garbage dumps. What Rio de Janeiro discards, Gramacho takes.

And what Gramacho takes, *catadores* scavenge. About three thousand garbage pickers scrape a living out of the rubbish, salvaging two hundred tons of recyclable scraps daily. They trail the never-ending convoy of trucks, trudging up the mountains of garbage and sliding down the other side, snagging scraps along the way. Plastic bottles, tubes, wires, and paper are sorted and sold to wholesalers who stand on the edge of the dump.

Across the bay the *Christ the Redeemer* statue extends his arms toward Rio's South Zone and its million-dollar beachfront apartments. Tourists flock there; no one comes to Gramacho. No one except Vik Muniz.

This Brazilian-born artist convinced five garbage workers to pose for individual portraits. Suelem, an eighteen-year-old mother of two, has worked the garbage since the age of seven. Isis is a recovering alcoholic and drug addict. Zumbi reads every book he finds in the trash. Irma cooks discarded produce in a large pot over an open fire and sells it. Tiao has organized the workers into an association.

Muniz took photos of their faces, then enlarged the images to the size of a basketball court. He and the five catadores outlined the facial features with trash. Bottle tops became eyebrows. Cardboard boxes became chin lines. Rubber tires overlaid shadows. Images gradually emerged from the trash. Muniz climbed onto a thirty-foot-tall platform and took new photos.

The result? The second-most-popular art exhibit in Brazilian history, exceeded only by the works of Picasso. Muniz donated the profits to the local garbage pickers' association.[4] You might say he treated Gramacho with grace.

Grace does this. God *does* this. Grace is God walking into your world with a sparkle in his eye and an offer that's hard to resist. "Sit still for a bit. I can do wonders with this mess of yours."

Believe this promise. Trust it. Cling like a barnacle to every hope and covenant.

—*Grace*

Grace

hugged the stink out of
the prodigal

and scared the hate out of Paul

and pledges to do the same in us.

Grace
comes after you.
It rewires you.

From insecure to God secure.

From regret-riddled to better-because-of-it.
From afraid-to-die to ready-to-fly.

I—YES, I ALONE—WILL BLOT OUT
YOUR SINS FOR MY OWN SAKE AND
WILL NEVER THINK OF THEM AGAIN.

Isaiah 43:25 NLT

AN OASIS OF GRACE

The cross of Christ creates a new people, a people unhindered by skin color or family feud. A new citizenry based not on common ancestry or geography, but on a common Savior.

My friend Buckner Fanning experienced this firsthand. He was a marine in World War II, stationed in Nagasaki three weeks after the dropping of the atomic bomb. Can you imagine a young American soldier amid the rubble and wreckage of the demolished city? Radiation-burned victims wandering the streets. Atomic fallout showering the city. Bodies burned to a casket black. Survivors shuffling through the streets, searching for family, food, and hope. The conquering soldier feeling not victory but grief for the suffering around him.

Instead of anger and revenge, Buckner found an oasis of grace. While patrolling the narrow streets, he came upon a sign that bore an English phrase: Methodist Church. He noted the location and resolved to return the next Sunday morning.

When he did, he entered a partially collapsed structure. Windows shattered. Walls buckled. The young marine stepped through the rubble, unsure how he would be received. Fifteen or so Japanese were setting up chairs and removing debris. When the uniformed American entered their midst, they stopped and turned.

He knew only one word in Japanese. He heard it. *Brother.* "They welcomed me as a friend," Buckner relates, the power of the moment still resonating more than sixty years after the events. They offered him a seat. He opened his Bible and, not understanding the sermon, sat and observed. During Communion the worshippers brought him the elements. In that quiet moment the enmity of their nations and the hurt of the war were set aside as one Christian served another the body and blood of Christ.

—Outlive Your Life

Through Christ we inherit
abundant mercy.
Enough to
cover a lifetime
of mistakes.

❧❧

Fear exhausting
God's grace?
A sardine will
swallow the
Atlantic first.

GOD, WITH UNDESERVED KINDNESS,
DECLARES THAT WE ARE RIGHTEOUS. HE
DID THIS THROUGH CHRIST JESUS WHEN
HE FREED US FROM THE PENALTY FOR
OUR SINS. FOR GOD PRESENTED JESUS
AS THE SACRIFICE FOR SIN. PEOPLE ARE
MADE RIGHT WITH GOD WHEN THEY
BELIEVE THAT JESUS SACRIFICED HIS LIFE,
SHEDDING HIS BLOOD.

Romans 3:24–25 NLT

God has **enough grace** to solve every dilemma you face, *wipe every tear* you cry, and **answer every question** you ask.

SHAPED

BY

Grace

Grace.

Let it so seep into
the crusty cracks
of your life that
everything softens.

Then let it bubble
to the surface, like a
spring in the Sahara,
in words of kindness
and deeds of generosity.

BE KIND TO
EACH OTHER,
TENDERHEARTED,
FORGIVING ONE
ANOTHER, JUST AS GOD
THROUGH CHRIST HAS
FORGIVEN YOU.

Ephesians 4:32 NLT

You will never be called upon
to give anyone more grace than
God has already given you.

THE GRACE-GIVEN, GIVE GRACE

Recently I shared a meal with some friends. A husband and wife wanted to tell me about a storm they were weathering. Through a series of events, she learned of an act of infidelity that had occurred over a decade ago. He had made the mistake of thinking it'd be better not to tell her, so he didn't. But she found out. And as you can imagine, she was deeply hurt.

Through the advice of a counselor, the couple dropped everything and went away for several days. A decision had to be made. Would they flee, fight, or forgive? So they prayed. They talked. They walked. They reflected. In this case the wife was clearly in the right. She could have left. Women have done so for lesser reasons. Or she could have stayed and made his life a living hell. Other women have done that. But she chose a different response.

On the tenth night of their trip, my friend found a card on his pillow. On the card was a printed verse: "I'd rather do nothing with you than something without you." Beneath the verse she had written these words:

I forgive you. I love you. Let's move on.

—*Just Like Jesus*

Grace is not blind.

It sees the hurt full well.
But grace chooses
to see God's forgiveness
even more.

GROW IN THE GRACE
AND KNOWLEDGE OF
OUR LORD AND SAVIOR
JESUS CHRIST.

2 Peter 3:18

My grace is sufficient
for you, for my power
is made perfect in
weakness.

2 Corinthians 12:9 NIV

You have God's Spirit
within you.

Heavenly hosts above you.
Jesus Christ interceding for you.

························· ❖❖ ·························

You have God's sufficient
grace to sustain you.

GRACE FOR EVERY NEED

The birth of our first child coincided with the cancellation of our health insurance. I still don't understand how it happened. It had to do with the company being based in the U.S. and Jenna being born in Brazil. Denalyn and I were left with the joy of an eight-pound baby girl and the burden of a twenty-five-hundred-dollar hospital bill.

We settled the bill by draining a savings account. Thankful to be able to pay the debt but bewildered by the insurance problem, I wondered, "Is God trying to tell us something?"

A few weeks later the answer came. I spoke at a retreat for a small, happy church in Florida. A member of the congregation handed me an envelope and said, "This is for your family." Such gifts were not uncommon. We were accustomed to and grateful for these unsolicited donations, which usually amounted to fifty or a hundred dollars. I expected the amount to be comparable. But when I opened the envelope, the check was for (you guessed it) twenty-five hundred dollars.

Through the language of need, God spoke to me. It was as if he said, "Max, I'm involved in your life. I will take care of you."

—He Chose the Nails

We indwell a garden of grace. God's love sprouts around us like lilacs and towers over us like Georgia pines.

CRY FOR HELP AND YOU'LL FIND IT'S GRACE AND MORE GRACE. THE MOMENT HE HEARS, HE'LL ANSWER.

Isaiah 30:19 MSG

God has resources we know nothing about, solutions outside our reality, provisions outside our possibility.

We see problems; God sees provision.

SHAPED BY GRACE

On a November evening in 2004, Victoria Ruvolo, a forty-four-year-old New Yorker, was driving to her home on Long Island. She'd just attended her niece's recital and was ready for the couch, a warm fire, and relaxation.

She doesn't remember seeing the silver Nissan approach from the east. She remembers nothing of the eighteen-year-old boy leaning out the window, holding, of all things, a frozen turkey. He threw it at her windshield.

The twenty-pound bird crashed through the glass, bent the steering wheel inward, and shattered her face like a dinner plate on concrete. The violent prank left her grappling for life in the ICU. She survived but only after doctors wired her jaw, affixed one eye by synthetic film, and bolted titanium plates to her cranium. She can't look in the mirror without a reminder of her hurt.[5]

Nine months after her disastrous November night, she stood face to titanium-bolted face with her offender in court. Ryan Cushing was no longer the cocky, turkey-tossing kid in the Nissan. He was trembling, tearful, and apologetic. For New York City, he had come to symbolize a generation of kids out of control. People packed the room to see him get his comeuppance. The judge's sentence enraged them—only six months behind bars, five years' probation, some counseling, and public service.

The courtroom erupted. Everyone objected. Everyone, that is, except Victoria Ruvolo. The reduced sentence was her idea. The boy walked over, and she embraced him. In full view of the judge and the crowd, she held him tight, stroked his hair. He sobbed, and she spoke: "I forgive you. I want your life to be the best it can be."[6]

She allowed grace to shape her response. "God gave me a second chance at life, and I passed it on," she says of her largesse.[7] "If I hadn't let go of that anger, I'd be consumed by this need for revenge. Forgiving him helps me move on."[8]

Her mishap led to her mission: volunteering with the county probation department. "I'm trying to help others, but I know for the rest of my life I'll be known as 'The Turkey Lady.' Could have been worse. He could have thrown a ham. I'd be Miss Piggy!"[9]

—*Grace*

This is the gift that
God gives: a grace that
grants us first the power
to receive love and then
the power to give it.

The grace-given
give grace.

⸙

Forgiven people
forgive people.

⸙

The mercy-marinated
drip mercy.

GOD IS KIND TO YOU SO YOU WILL
CHANGE YOUR HEARTS AND LIVES.

Romans 2:4 NCV

SUCH KINDNESS

"We will celebrate forty-four years tomorrow," Jack said, feeding his wife.

She was bald. Her eyes were sunken, and her speech was slurred. She looked straight ahead, only opening her mouth when he brought the fork near. He wiped her cheek. He wiped his brow.

"She has been sick for five years," he told me. "She can't walk. She can't take care of herself. She can't even feed herself, but I love her. And," he spoke louder so she could hear, "we are going to beat this thing, aren't we, Honey?"

He fed her a few bites and spoke again, "We don't have insurance. When I could afford it, I thought I wouldn't need it. Now I owe this hospital more than $50,000." He was quiet for a few moments as he gave her a drink. Then he continued. "But they don't pester me. They know I can't pay, but they admitted us with no questions asked. The doctors treat us like we are their best-paying patients. Who would've imagined such kindness?"

I had to agree with him. Who would've imagined such kindness? In a thorny world of high-tech, expensive, often criticized health care, it was reassuring to find professionals who would serve two who had nothing to give in return.

—*In the Eye of the Storm*

One of the best ways to
celebrate God's amazing love
and grace is to share some of
that love and grace with others.

GOD MADE HIM WHO
HAD NO SIN TO BE SIN
FOR US, SO THAT IN HIM
WE MIGHT BECOME THE
RIGHTEOUSNESS OF GOD.

2 Corinthians 5:21

A GRACE-FILLED LOVE

The voices yanked her out of bed.

"Get up, you harlot."

Priests slammed open the bedroom door, threw back the window curtains, and pulled off the covers. Before she felt the warmth of the morning sun, she felt the heat of their scorn.

"Shame on you."

She scarcely had time to cover her body before they marched her through the narrow streets. Dogs yelped. Roosters ran. Women leaned out their windows. Mothers snatched children off the path. . . .

And as if the bedroom raid and parade of shame were inadequate, the men thrust her into the middle of a morning Bible class.

Early the next morning [Jesus] was back again at the Temple. . . . As he was speaking, the teachers of religious law and the Pharisees brought a woman who had been caught in the act of adultery. They put her in front of the crowd.

"Teacher," they said to Jesus, "this woman was caught in the very of adultery. The law of Moses says to stone her. What do you say?" (John 8:2–5 NLT).

Stunned students stood on one side of her. Pious plaintiffs on the other. They had their questions and convictions; she had her dangling negligee and smeared lipstick. "This woman was caught in the act of adultery," her accusers crowed. . . . "The law of Moses says to stone her. What do you say?"

The woman had no exit. Deny the accusation? She had been caught. Plead for mercy? From whom? From

God? His spokesmen were squeezing stones and snarling their lips. No one would speak for her.

But someone would stoop for her.

Jesus "stooped down and wrote in the dust" (v. 6 NLT). We would expect him to stand up, step forward, or even ascend a stair and speak. But instead he leaned over. He descended lower than anyone else—beneath the priests, the people, even beneath the woman. . . .

He's prone to stoop. . . . He stooped before the Roman whipping post. Stooped to carry the cross. Grace is a God who stoops. Here he stooped to write in the sand. . . .

The posse grew impatient with the silent, stooping Jesus. "They kept demanding an answer, so he stood up" (v. 7 NLT).

He lifted himself erect until his shoulders were straight and his head was high. . . . He stood on behalf of the woman. He placed himself between her and the lynch mob and said, "'All right, [stone her,] but let the one who has never sinned throw the first stone!' Then he stooped down again and wrote in the dust" (vv. 7–8 NLT).

Name-callers shut their mouths. Rocks fell to the ground. Jesus resumed his scribbling. "When the accusers heard this, they slipped away one by one, beginning with the oldest, until only Jesus was left in the middle of the crowd with the woman" (v. 9 NLT).

Jesus wasn't finished. He stood one final time and asked the woman, . . . "Where are your accusers? Didn't even one of them condemn you?"

"No, Lord," she said.

And Jesus said, "Neither do I. Go and sin no more" (John 8:10–11 NLT).

Within a few moments the courtyard was empty. Jesus, the woman, her critics—they all left. But let's linger. Look at the rocks on the ground, abandoned and unused. And look at the scribbling in the sand. It's the only sermon Jesus ever wrote. While we don't know the words, I'm wondering if they read like this:

Grace happens here.

—*Grace*

BEING MADE RIGHT
WITH GOD BY HIS
GRACE, WE COULD
HAVE THE HOPE OF
RECEIVING THE LIFE
THAT NEVER ENDS.

Titus 3:7 NCV

When you love the
unloving, you get
a glimpse of what
God does for you.

When you keep the porch light on for the prodigal child, when you do what is right even though you have been done wrong, when you love the weak and the sick, you do what God does every single moment.

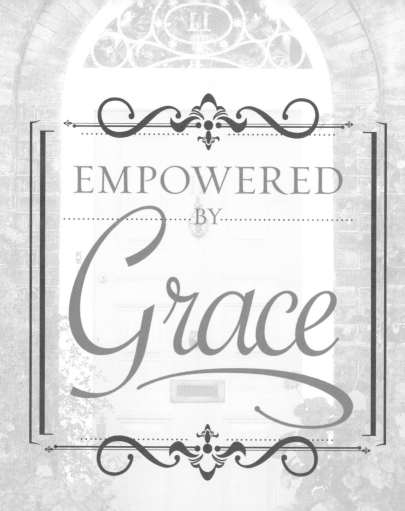

EMPOWERED
BY
Grace

God is the great giver.
The great provider.

······· ❦❦ ·······

The fount of every blessing.

Absolutely generous and
utterly dependable.

We dare to stake *our hope* on the gladdest news of all:

if God permits the challenge, he will *provide the grace to meet it.*

He who did not spare his own Son, but
gave him up for us all—how will he
not also, along with him, graciously
give us all things?

Romans 8:32

GOD USES PEOPLE LIKE YOU AND ME

God changes the world with folks like you.

Just ask the twenty-two people who traveled to London on a fall morning in 2009 to thank Nicholas Winton. They could have passed for a retirement-home social club. All were in their seventies or eighties. More gray hair than not. More shuffled steps than quick ones.

But this was no social trip. It was a journey of gratitude. They came to thank the man who had saved their lives: a stooped centenarian who met them on a train platform just as he had in 1939.

He was a twenty-nine-year-old stockbroker at the time. Hitler's armies were ravaging the nation of Czechoslovakia, tearing Jewish families apart and marching parents to concentration camps. No one was caring for the children. Winton got wind of their plight and resolved to help them. He used his vacation to travel to Prague, where he met parents who, incredibly, were willing to entrust their children's future to his care. After returning to England, he worked his regular job on the stock exchange by day and advocated for the children at night. He convinced Great Britain to permit their entry. He found foster homes and raised funds. Then he scheduled his first transport on March 14, 1939, and accomplished seven more over the next five months. His last trainload of children arrived on August 2, bringing the total of rescued children to 669.

On September 1, the biggest transport was to take place, but Hitler invaded Poland, and Germany closed borders throughout Europe. None of the 250 children on that train were ever seen again.

After the war Winton didn't tell anyone of his rescue efforts, not even his wife. In 1988 she found a scrapbook in their attic with all the children's photos and a complete list of names. She prodded him to tell the story. As he has, rescued children have returned to say thank you. The grateful group includes a film director, a Canadian journalist, a news correspondent, a former minister in the British cabinet, a magazine manager, and one of the founders of the Israeli Air Force. There are some seven thousand children, grandchildren, and great-grandchildren who owe their existence to Winton's bravery. He wears a ring given to him by some of the children he saved. It bears a line from the Talmud, the book of Jewish law: "Save one life. Save the world."[10]

—Outlive Your Life

Do you know God's grace?

Then you can love boldly, live robustly.

Nothing fosters courage like a clear grasp of grace.

Give grace, one more time.
Be generous, one more time.

EACH ONE SHOULD USE
WHATEVER GIFT HE
HAS RECEIVED TO SERVE
OTHERS, FAITHFULLY
ADMINISTERING GOD'S
GRACE IN ITS VARIOUS
FORMS.

1 Peter 4:10

REACHING OUT IN LOVE

Jesus told the story of an affluent white man who was driving home from his downtown office. Since the hour was late and he was tired, he took the direct route, which led through the roughest part of the city. Wouldn't you know it—he ran out of gas. While walking to the convenience store, he was mugged and left for dead on the sidewalk.

A few minutes later a preacher drove by on the way to the evening service. He saw the man on the sidewalk and started to help but then realized it would be too dangerous to stop.

Soon thereafter a respected community leader came by and saw the man but decided it was best not to get involved.

Finally, an old Hispanic immigrant driving a beat-up truck saw the man, stopped, and took him to the hospital. He paid the hospital bill and went on his way.

I altered the characters but not Jesus' question: "Which . . . was a neighbor to the man?" (Luke 10:36). Your neighbor is not just the person in the next house but the one in the next block or ghetto. Your neighbor is the person you've been taught not to love. For the Jew in the days of Jesus, it was a Samaritan.

For an Israeli today, it is a Palestinian.

For an Arab, a Jew.

For a black male, how about a pickup-driving, gun-toting, tobacco-chewing, baseball cap–wearing redneck?

For the Hispanic poor, how about the Hispanic afflu-ent? For any Hispanic, how about the person who called you "wetback"?

For the white, the one who called you "gringo."

And for the black, the one who called you "boy."

Loving your neighbor is loving the person you used to hate.

—Max on Life

If God allows me with my foibles and failures to call him

Father,

shouldn't I extend the same grace to others?

I WAS SHOWN MERCY SO THAT
IN ME, THE WORST OF SINNERS,
CHRIST JESUS MIGHT DISPLAY
HIS UNLIMITED PATIENCE AS
AN EXAMPLE FOR THOSE WHO
WOULD BELIEVE ON HIM AND
RECEIVE ETERNAL LIFE.

1 Timothy 1:16

If God so loved us, can
we not love one another?
Having been forgiven,
can we not forgive?

Having feasted at the
table of grace, can we not
share a few crumbs?

GOD MEETS OUR NEEDS WITH GRACE

Heather Sample suspected trouble the moment she saw the cut on her father's hand. The two had sat down for a quick lunch between surgical procedures. Heather spotted the wound and asked him about it. When Kyle explained that the injury had happened during an operation, a wave of nausea swept over her.

Both were doctors. Both knew the risk. Both understood the danger of treating AIDS patients in Zimbabwe. And now their fears were realized.

Kyle Sheets was a twelve-year veteran of medical mission trips. . . . This trip to Zimbabwe was not his first.

Exposure to the AIDS virus was.

Heather urged her father to immediately begin the antiretroviral treatment in order to prevent HIV infection. Kyle was reluctant. He knew the side effects. Each was life threatening. Still, Heather insisted, and he consented. Within hours he was violently ill. . . .

They moved up their departure time as they began to wonder if Kyle would survive the forty-hour trip, which included a twelve-hour layover in South Africa and a seventeen-hour flight to Atlanta.

Kyle boarded the transoceanic plane with a 104.5° fever. He shook with chills. By this time he was having trouble breathing and was unable to sit up. Incoherent. Eyes yellowed. Liver enlarged and painful. Both doctors recognized the symptoms of acute liver failure. Heather felt the full weight of her father's life on her shoulders.

Heather explained the situation to the pilots and convinced them that her father's best hope was the fastest flight possible to the United States. Having only a stethoscope and a vial of epinephrine, she took her seat next to his and wondered how she would pull his body into the aisle to do CPR if his heart stopped.

Several minutes into the flight Kyle drifted off to sleep. Heather crawled over him and made it to the bathroom in time to vomit the water she had just drunk. She slumped on the floor in a fetal position, wept, and prayed, *I need help.*

Heather doesn't remember how long she prayed, but it was long enough for a concerned passenger to knock on the door. She opened it to see four men standing in the galley. One asked if she was okay. Heather assured him that she was fine and told him that she was a doctor. His face brightened as he explained that he and his three friends were physicians too. "And so are ninety-six other passengers!" he said. One hundred physicians from Mexico were on the flight.

Heather explained the situation and asked for their help and prayers. They gave both. They alerted a colleague who was a top-tier infectious disease doctor. Together they evaluated Kyle's condition and agreed that nothing else could be done.

They offered to watch him so she could rest. She did. When she awoke, Kyle was standing and talking to one of the doctors. Though still ICU-level sick, he was much stronger. Heather began to recognize God's hand at work. He had placed them on exactly the right plane with exactly the right people. God had met their need with grace.

—*Grace*

You are a trophy of God's kindness, a partaker of his mission. Not perfect by any means but closer to perfection than you've ever been. Steadily stronger, gradually better. This happens when grace happens.

The dynamic of giving
grace is the key to
understanding grace,

for it is when we forgive

others that we begin to

feel what God feels.

See your enemy as God's child and revenge as God's job.

How can we grace-recipients do anything less? Dare we ask God for grace when we refuse to give it?

A GIFT OF GRACE

After we'd been in San Antonio only a short time, I decided I should buy a new jacket for Easter. Where we served in Brazil, no one wore coats and ties, so I didn't have many. Hence, I went to buy one. At the rack I realized I was standing next to a well-known citizen, Red McCombs. He owns car lots and at one time owned an NFL football team in Minnesota.

We exchanged greetings and niceties. He told me about his brother, a pastor. I told him how happy I was to be living in San Antonio. After a moment we returned to our shopping. I selected a jacket, went to pay for it, and was told these words: "Your jacket has already been paid for. The man you were talking to covered your bill." My first thought was, *Boy, I wish I'd picked out some slacks too.*

Think about what happened to me. I was in debt. Then, all of a sudden, I found that my debt had been paid. I could deny the gift or accept it. The decision was easy. The gift giver had ample resources with which to pay for the coat. I had no reason to doubt his sincerity or ability.

Nor do you. God has ample ability to love and care for you.

—Max on Life

The merciful,
says Jesus,
are shown mercy.

They witness grace.

They are blessed because they
are testimonies to a greater goodness.

God's blessings are
dispensed according to the

riches of his grace,

not according to the

depth of our faith.

BEING CONFIDENT OF THIS,
THAT HE WHO BEGAN A GOOD
WORK IN YOU WILL CARRY IT
ON TO COMPLETION UNTIL THE
DAY OF CHRIST JESUS.

Philippians 1:6

GIVING

Grace

*When grace happens,
generosity happens.*

*Unsquashable,
eye-popping
bigheartedness
happens.*

Receiving grace today?

Liberality is in the forecast for tomorrow.

A KISS OF KINDNESS

My friend Kenny and his family had just returned from Disney World. "I saw a sight I'll never forget," he said. "I want you to know about it."

He and his family were inside Cinderella's castle. It was packed with kids and parents. Suddenly all the children rushed to one side. Had it been a boat, the castle would have tipped over. Cinderella had entered.

Cinderella. The pristine princess. Kenny said she was perfectly typecast. A gorgeous young girl with each hair in place, flawless skin, and a beaming smile. She stood waist-deep in a garden of kids, each wanting to touch and be touched.

For some reason Kenny turned and looked toward the other side of the castle. It was now vacant except for a boy maybe seven or eight years old. His age was hard to determine because of the disfigurement of his body.

Dwarfed in height, face deformed, he stood watching quietly and wistfully, holding the hand of an older brother.

Don't you know what he wanted? He wanted to be with the children. He longed to be in the middle of the kids reaching for Cinderella, calling her name. But can't you feel his fear, fear of yet another rejection? Fear of being taunted again, mocked again?

Don't you wish Cinderella would go to him? Guess what? She did!

She noticed the little boy. She immediately began walking in his direction. Politely but firmly inching through the crowd of children, she finally broke free. She walked quickly across the floor, knelt at eye level with the stunned little boy, and placed a kiss on his face.

—*A Gentle Thunder*

When you meet a bountiful person, you are standing where grace is happening.

THE GRACE OF
GOD THAT BRINGS
SALVATION HAS
APPEARED TO ALL MEN.

Titus 2:11

CASCADING GRACE

Amy Wells knew her bridal shop would be busy. Brides-to-be took full advantage of the days right after Thanksgiving. It was common for a cluster of in-laws and siblings to spend the better part of the holiday weekend looking at wedding dresses in her San Antonio, Texas, store. . . .

Across town Jack Autry was in the hospital, struggling to stay alive. He was in the final stages of melanoma. He had collapsed two days before and had been rushed to the emergency room. His extended family was in town not just to celebrate Thanksgiving together but to make preparations for his daughter's wedding. Chrysalis was only months from marriage. The women in the family had planned to spend the day selecting a wedding gown. But now with Jack in the hospital, Chrysalis didn't want to go.

Jack insisted. After much persuasion, Chrysalis, her mother, her future mother-in-law, and her sisters went to the bridal salon. The shop owner noticed that the women were a bit subdued, but she assumed this was just a quiet family. She helped Chrysalis try on dress after dress until she found an ivory duchess silk and satin gown that everyone loved. Jack was fond of calling Chrysalis his princess, and the dress, Chrysalis commented, made her look just like one.

That's when Amy heard about Jack. Because of the cancer, he couldn't come see his daughter in her dress. And because of the medical bills, the family couldn't buy the dress yet. It appeared that Jack Autry would die without seeing his daughter dressed as a bride.

Amy would hear nothing of it. She told Chrysalis to take the gown and veil to the hospital and wear it for her daddy. She says, "I knew it was fine. There was no doubt in my mind to do this. God was talking to me." No credit card was requested or given. Amy didn't even make note of a phone number. She urged the family to go directly to the hospital. Chrysalis didn't have to be told twice.

When she arrived at her father's room, he was heavily medicated and asleep. As family members woke him, the doors to the room slowly opened, and there he saw his daughter, engulfed in fifteen yards of layered, billowing silk. He was able to stay alert for about twenty seconds.

"But those twenty seconds were magical," Chrysalis remembers. "My daddy saw me walk in wearing the most beautiful dress. He was really weak. He smiled and just kept looking at me. I held his hand, and he held mine. I asked him if I looked like a princess . . . He nodded. He looked at me a little more, and it almost looked like he was about to cry. And then he went to sleep."

Three days later he died.[11]

Amy's generosity created a moment of cascading grace. God to Amy to Chrysalis to Jack.

Isn't this how it works?

—*Grace*

Jesus
was God's model of
a human being.

Ever honest in the midst of hypocrisy.

Relentlessly kind in a world of cruelty.

THE LORD'S LOVE NEVER ENDS; HIS MERCIES
NEVER STOP. THEY ARE NEW EVERY MORNING.

Lamentations 3:22—23 NCV

GRACE GIVEN TO ALL

Some years back a reporter covering the conflict in Sarajevo saw a little girl shot by a sniper. The back of her head had been torn away by the bullet. The reporter threw down his pad and pencil and stopped being a reporter for a few minutes. He rushed to the man who was holding the child and helped them both into his car. As the reporter stepped on the accelerator, racing to the hospital, the man holding the bleeding child said, "Hurry, my friend. My child is still alive."

A moment or two later he pleaded, "Hurry, my friend. My child is still breathing."

A moment later, "Hurry, my friend. My child is still warm."

Finally, "Hurry. Oh my God, my child is getting cold."

By the time they arrived at the hospital, the little girl had died. As the two men were in the lavatory, washing the blood off their hands and their clothes, the man turned to the reporter and said, "This is a terrible task for me. I must go tell her father that his child is dead. He will be heartbroken."

The reporter was amazed. He looked at the grieving man and said, "I thought she was your child."

The man looked back and said, "No, but aren't they all our children?"[12]

—*Outlive Your Life*

How can we,
who have been
loved so much,
not do the same
for others?

GRACE TEACHES US TO
LIVE IN THE PRESENT
AGE IN A WISE AND
RIGHT WAY AND IN A
WAY THAT SHOWS WE
SERVE GOD.

Titus 2:12 NCV

Because God has
forgiven us, we
can forgive others.

❦

Because he has a forgiving heart,
we can have a forgiving heart.
We can have a heart like his.

Whatever you do,
whether in word or
deed, do it all in the
name of the Lord
Jesus, giving thanks
to God the Father
through him.

Colossians 3:17

A SONG IN THE HEART

Barbara Leininger and her sister, Regina, were daughters of German immigrants who had settled in Colonial Pennsylvania, and the two girls were eleven and nine years old when they were kidnapped. On a fall day in 1755, the sisters were in the farm cabin with their brother and father when two Indian warriors slammed open the door.... Their father offered the Indians food and tobacco. He told the girls to fetch a bucket of water, that the men must be thirsty. As the girls scurried out the door, he spoke to them in German and told them not to come back until the Indians were gone. They raced toward the nearby creek....

Later the Indians found the girls hiding in the grass and dragged them away.... Days became weeks as the Indians marched the captives westward. Barbara did her best to stay close to Regina and keep up her spirits. She reminded Regina of the song their mother had taught them:

Alone, yet not alone am I
Though in this solitude so drear
I feel my Savior always nigh.[13]

At a certain point, the Indians dispersed, separating the sisters. . . . The two girls were marched in opposite directions. Barbara's journey continued several weeks, deeper and deeper into the forest. . . . She lost all contact with her family and fellow settlers.

Three years later Barbara escaped. She ran through the woods for eleven days, finally reaching safety at Fort Pitt. . . . No one had news of Regina.

Barbara thought daily of her sister, but her hope had no substance until six years later. She had married and had begun raising her own family when she received word that 206 captives had been rescued and taken to Fort Carlisle. Might Regina be one of them?

Barbara and her mother set off to find out. The sight of the refugees stunned them. Most had spent years isolated in villages, separated from any settlers. They were emaciated and confused. They were so pale they blended in with the snow.

Barbara and her mother walked up and down the line, calling Regina's name, searching faces and speaking German. No one looked or spoke back. The mother and daughter turned away with tears in their eyes and told the colonel that Regina wasn't among the rescued.

The colonel urged them to be sure. He asked about identifying blemishes such as scars or birthmarks. There were none. He asked about heirlooms, a necklace or bracelet. The mother shook her head. Regina had been wearing no jewelry. The colonel had one final idea: was there a childhood memory or song?

The faces of the two women brightened. What about the song they sang each night? Barbara and her mother immediately turned and began to walk slowly up and down the rows. As they walked, they sang, "Alone, yet not alone am I . . ." For a long time no one responded. . . . Then all of a sudden Barbara heard a loud cry. A tall, slender girl rushed out of the crowd toward her mother, embraced her, and began to sing the verse.

Regina had not recognized her mother or sister. She had forgotten how to speak English and German. But she remembered the song that had been placed in her heart as a young girl.[14]

God places a song in the hearts of his children too. A song of hope and life. "He put a new song in my mouth" (Psalm 40:3).

—*Grace*

YOU GAVE ME LIFE AND SHOWED ME
KINDNESS, AND IN YOUR CARE YOU
WATCHED OVER MY LIFE.

Job 10:12 NCV

The mercy of Christ preceded our mistakes;

❖❖

our mercy must precede the mistakes of others.

GOD IS ABLE TO MAKE ALL
GRACE ABOUND TOWARD YOU,
THAT YOU, ALWAYS HAVING ALL
SUFFICIENCY IN ALL THINGS,
MAY HAVE AN ABUNDANCE FOR
EVERY GOOD WORK.

2 Corinthians 9:8 NKJV

Saving grace saves us
from our sins.

Sustaining grace
meets us at our point of need
and equips us with

courage, wisdom,

and strength.

GOD'S HEALING GRACE

She had been bleeding for twelve years. By the time she got to Jesus, she had nothing left. The doctors had taken her last dime. The diagnosis had stolen her last hope. And the hemorrhage had robbed her of her last drop of energy. She had no more money, no more friends, and no more options. With the end of her rope in one hand and a wing and a prayer in her heart, she shoved her way through the crowd.

When her hand touched his garment, a transfusion occurred. He let it go out and she let it go in.

It didn't bother Jesus that the woman came to him as a last resort. To him it mattered only that she came. He knows that with some of us it takes a lot of reality to snap us to our senses, so he doesn't keep a time clock. Those who scramble in at quitting time get the same wage as those who beat the morning whistle. I guess that's what makes grace, grace.

—*God Came Near*

*God does not give us
what we deserve.
He has drenched his
world in grace.*

To whom does God offer
his gift of grace?

To the brightest? The
most beautiful or the
most charming?

No.

His gift is for us all—
beggars and bankers,
clergy and clerks,
judges and janitors.

All God's children.

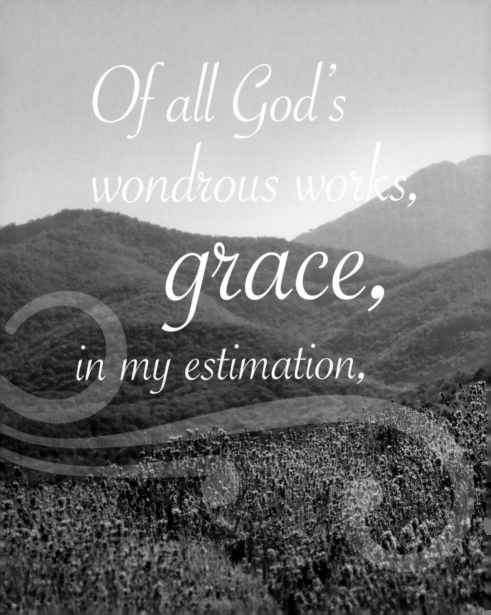

Of all God's wondrous works,

grace,

in my estimation,

is the

magnum

opus.

ENDNOTES

1. John Bishop, *1041 Sermon Illustrations, Ideas, and Expositions*, ed. A. Gordon Nasby (Grand Rapids: Baker Book House, 1952), 213.

2. Jim Reimann, *Victor Hugo's Les Misérables* (Nashville, TN: Word Publishing, 2001), 16.

3. Ibid., 29–31.

4. "Rio de Janeiro's Garbage Workers Make Art-Project Out of Trash," Street News Service, May 2, 2011, www.streetnewsservice.org/news/2011/may/feed-278/rio-de-janeiro%E2%80%99s-garbage-workers-make-art-project-out-of-trash.aspx.

5. David Jeremiah, *Captured by Grace: No One Is Beyond the Reach of a Loving God* (Nashville: Thomas Nelson, 2006), 9–10.

6. Ibid., 11.

7. Robin Finn, "Pushing Past the Trauma to Forgiveness," *New York Times*, October 28, 2005, www.nytimes.com/2005/10/28/nyregion/28lives.html.

8. Jonathan Lemire, "Victoria Ruvolo, Who Was Hit by Turkey Nearly 6 Years Ago, Forgives Teens for Terrible Prank," *New York Daily News*, November 7, 2010, http://articles.nydailynews.com/2010-11-07/local/27080547_1_victoria-ruvolo-ryan-cushing-forgives.

9. Ibid.

10. "Nicholas Winton, the Power of Good," Gelman Educational Foundation, www.powerofgood.net/story.php, and Patrick D. Odum, "Gratitude

That Costs Us Something," *Heartlight*, www.heartlight.org/cgi/simplify
.cgi?20090922_gratitude.html.

11. Michael Quintanilla, "Angel Gives Dying Father Wedding Moment," *San Antonio Express-News*, December 15, 2010. Used by permission of Chrysalis Autry.

12. Sam Nunn, "Intellectual Honesty, Moral and Ethical Behavior; We Must Decide What Is Important" (speech, National Prayer Breakfast, Washington, DC, February 1, 1996).

13. Tracy Leininger Craven, *Alone, Yet Not Alone* (San Antonio, TX: His Seasons, 2001), 19.

14. Ibid., 29–31, 42, 153–54, 176, 190–97.

SOURCES

All of the material in this book was originally
published in the following books by Max
Lucado. All copyrights to the original works
are held by the author, Max Lucado.

In the Eye of the Storm (Nashville: Thomas Nelson, Inc., 1991).

A Gentle Thunder (Nashville: Thomas Nelson, Inc., 1995).

In the Grip of Grace (Nashville: Thomas Nelson, Inc., 1996).

The Great House of God (Nashville: Thomas Nelson, Inc., 1997).

Just Like Jesus (Nashville: Thomas Nelson, Inc., 1998).

He Chose the Nails (Nashville: Thomas Nelson, Inc., 2000).

And the Angels Were Silent (Nashville: Thomas Nelson, Inc., 2003).

God Came Near (Nashville: Thomas Nelson, Inc., 2003).

It's Not About Me (Nashville: Thomas Nelson, Inc., 2004).

Cure for the Common Life (Nashville: Thomas Nelson, Inc., 2005).

Facing Your Giants (Nashville: Thomas Nelson, Inc., 2006).

3:16, Numbers of Hope (Nashville: Thomas Nelson, Inc., 2007).

Outlive Your Life (Nashville: Thomas Nelson, Inc., 2010).

Max on Life (Nashville: Thomas Nelson, Inc., 2010).

Grace (Nashville: Thomas Nelson, Inc., 2012).

ENJOY THESE OTHER PRODUCTS ABOUT GRACE BY MAX...

Grace (Trade):

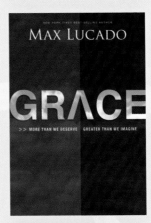

978-0-8499-2070-7

Wild Grace (Teen):

978-1-4003-2084-4

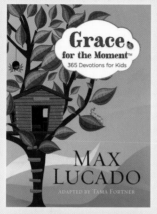

978-1-4003-2034-9

Grace for the Moment for Kids:

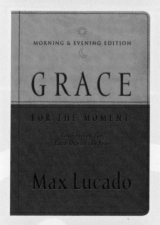

978-1-4041-9006-1

*Grace for the Moment
Morning & Evening:*

Jesus already knows the cost of grace. He already knows the price of forgiveness. But he offers it anyway.